Jean Cocteau

by

WILLIAM FIFIELD

 **Columbia University Press**

NEW YORK & LONDON 1974

COLUMBIA ESSAYS ON MODERN WRITERS
is a series of critical studies of English,
Continental, and other writers whose works are of contemporary
artistic and intellectual significance.

Editor

George Stade

Advisory Editors

Jacques Barzun   W. T. H. Jackson   Joseph A. Mazzeo

Jean Cocteau is Number 70 of the series

WILLIAM FIFIELD
has written several novels, including
The Devil's Marchioness and *The Sign of Taurus,*
as well as short stories and articles.
His *Jean Cocteau par Jean Cocteau: Entretiens avec
William Fifield* was published by Editions Stock
in Paris last year, and a recording of one of his
conversations with Jean Cocteau has been issued by
Caedmon Records as *Jean Cocteau, a Self-Portrait.*

Library of Congress Cataloging in Publication Data

Fifield, William, 1916–
  Jean Cocteau.

  (Columbia essays on modern writers, no. 70)
Bibliography: p. 47–48
1. Cocteau, Jean, 1889–1963—Criticism and inter-
pretation. I. Series.
PQ2605.015Z682   848'.9'1209   74-1173
ISBN 0-231-03369-9

Jean Cocteau

Jean Cocteau, toward the end of his life, concluded that genius was an unknown form of the memory. Saying that man was born with a monkey on one shoulder and a parrot on the other, he felt he sufficiently accounted for process in creative art. He had, then, to account for originality. He said (with Picasso and others of the Paris School) that it resulted from *error.* By the end of the second decade of the century, he had formulated the dictum which, apocryphally or not, he attributed in essence to his young friend Raymond Radiguet: "The genius tries to do what others do and fails." It remained to determine why the genius kept the failure. Deep brooding on this brought him, shortly before his death in 1963, to the disorienting belief that the genius, remembering forward across contiguous time, which Cocteau called the *intemporel,* stopped at the point at which it would subsequently prove he had stopped.

The use Cocteau made of ideas of this sort, which were essentially articles of faith, is revealing. In *The Impromptu of the Palais-Royal,* a curtain-raiser for the Comédie-Française published the year before his death, the action takes place in nontime, but hardly the nontime of science fiction. We find Molière lunching with Louis XIV and discussing such things as the scandal of Cocteau's last full-length play, *Bacchus* (1951), on which François Mauriac walked out. We may interpret the *spectatrice* who constantly and disrespectfully interrupts from the audience as an instance of stage technique, of which Cocteau was too much past master for his own good, except, finally, in one way, or as mockery of the play, evidence of a much deeper reflex of the spirit.

[3]

If *The Impromptu of the Palais-Royal* seems to us marred, exactly as was his first play *Orpheus* thirty-seven years earlier, by the graceless intrusion of C.O.C.T.E.A.U. (see page 32), in the earlier play significantly as "the accused," and in the later as the mocked author, what strikes us more is that he does convey his sadness at the use of bad taste. He felt, not without reason, that "bad taste" was necessary to the art of the twentieth century, and his particular quality, found so pervasively in no other, stems from the fact that he regretted it. He was in advance of currents which are just now surfacing—he obeyed, and deplored—and it may be to this more than to overt rebellion and to homosexuality, blazons of freedom carried reluctantly except in sex about which he was amusing by being delicately oblique, that is owed his increasing relevancy. A decade has passed since his death, and, unlike any other French writer of his period, his image is more alive in the public mind, in France, than when he was alive.

It is strange, because his presence was considered to be the cause of his fame. "Reading his plays, he projects into them the fire of his spirit. Away from his presence, they lose their color—like road marker buttons which cease to glitter when the car has passed." Written in 1943 in *Theatre of the Mad Years,* this expressed the prevalent opinion. And yet his works seem to have metamorphosed with his death.

There were, in fact, evidences at the time. In the late 1930s, he was taxed with being the cause of immorality and French youth-in-revolt. But few saw that his novel *Les Enfants Terribles* (published in 1929, but taking its effect with slow momentum through a decade) indeed was the very text for the sentiment to come: "my own closed (somewhat incestuous) world and to the devil with yours." His popularity was reduced by an ambiguous position during the war: though two of his plays, in particular *Les Parents Terribles,* were banned as immoral by the puri-

[4]

tanical German Occupation, a certain "aroma" attached to him which caused him to remark ruefully later, "That I happen to like a large blond soldier does not necessarily make me a Nazi, does it?" Meanwhile, underground, something else was going on—perhaps it was merely that time was catching him up. A surprisingly long time ago, he had expressed the total loneliness of the anarchist position of whole freedom to which contemporary creation has won, and it is perhaps the wistfulness and delicate irony of his advocacy that gives him increasing currency. His diffidence caused him to take what he thought a truth, toss it in the air, and by legerdemain (aptest of words when taken apart in its original French) make it come down as a dove. The apostle of unreason now appears to have possessed reason of the senses, so that he had all along for us what progressively seems to be all that is left us.

Cocteau was born in Maisons-Laffitte near Paris. It is important that he was raised by women. He was ten when his father, Georges Cocteau, died—an age he ordinarily somewhat reduced, in the telling. He was raised Lecomte, by his mother Eugénie Lecomte. He once told me he could not account for his artistic origins, for "there was no artistic talent in my family"; but in fact his father was a painter of excellent if unambitious accomplishment, and his maternal grandfather, Eugène Lecomte (the monsters of his later invention on the verge of World War I were to be called Eugènes), was an amateur chamber musician and owner of Stradivaris.

He was indeed a fabulist, but in part this was an aspect of an exquisite courtesy, almost of love—he knew well what details were useful, to enchant, to amuse, to lighten the burden of a world become too literal. Viewed in this way the charge that he was a prestidigitator, even liar, constantly leveled against him in life, seems undiscerning and actually wide of the mark.

Perusal of his twenty volumes of *critique*, essays, reports of every description in which he frequently analyzes himself, will show him a most unreliable witness on the surface, errant in facts, dates, attribution of quotations, yet at the same time there gradually emerges a different visage—the victim. This is probably how he saw himself. When I talked to him, the suggestion was in his voice—more expressive than his words, and often running counter to what he said. Extroversion, vulnerability to the human contagion, deeply sexually rooted and having verbalist roots, shut him from the position he shared with many artists since Rimbaud—turning one's back on art. He could not, because this meant turning one's back on friends; and, to be just, meant stifling an extraordinary articulateness. A peculiar articulateness, nonetheless. Conversation was his love—and writing "agonizing." Of his writing he has attested that his apparent facility was really the result of "a ferocious mathematical calculation"; and then, characteristically contradicting himself, has attested elsewhere that he never wrote unless he had "received orders" and that writing was an unconscious process of "exhalation" (by which he meant to differentiate between inspiration, which he considered trite, and expiration—the exhaling of the self into the work, necessarily autobiographical at all times whether one intended it or not).

He was "seventeen" when his poems were given a public reading at the Fémina Theatre on the Champs-Elysées under the aegis of the then leading actor of the day, de Max, and (this is apocryphal and part of the legend he sustained) Sarah Bernhardt. The reading was on April 4, 1908. Since he was born in July, 1889, he was then three months short of nineteen—yet he was "seventeen." It was not entirely his poetic ability which recommended him to de Max, and a system started which, in reverse, was to play throughout his life, his own famous ephebes being Radiguet, Jean Genet, and Jean Marais. He quickly be-

[6]

came the darling of a segment of Paris, friend of Marcel Proust, Edmond Rostand, yet it is the brevity of this period which seems significant as we look back. Always averring that the example of Gide had made him ashamed, he did evade, in a surprisingly short three or four years, the role of *The Frivolous Prince* (1910) and Aladdin of *Aladdin's Lamp* (1909)—first books of poems he later suppressed and, with *The Dance of Sophocles* (1912), omitted from his collected works. It was not in fact Gide until later but a critic for the *Nouvelle Revue Française* who, giving him a very thorough rating, elsewhere aptly observed that "they wouldn't let him go until he agreed to play their child genius"— yet *Gide*, for, from the outset, he had his infallible instinct for Names.

He tells us that the crucial influence was Stravinsky. There were in fact four or five crucial turns, their common sign seeming, as we can look with perspective, a need to submit. Certainly he felt extinguished by any position he had gained. Suffocated. And perhaps it is for this that we more and more find him authentic. Had, he has written, he met Picasso before 1916, when the outrage of *Les Demoiselles d'Avignon* was already nine years in the past, it would have been the Spaniard who taught him that, in his words, art was a sacerdocy to which you had to submit. As it befell, it was the Russian. He commenced to frequent the Ballet Russe and Diaghilev almost from their arrival, and the next year, 1911, he designed a poster for Diaghilev, thus taking up the tradition from Toulouse-Lautrec that posters were chic art, and commencing to exercise a manual dexterity he never took very seriously.

The Blue God, in 1912, he eventually suppressed too, but this ballet, danced by Nijinsky, was at least his first cohesive work. This inauspicious venture harked back; not until 1921 would he hark forward, but then with a depressing leap that brought him alongside the Ionesco of *The Bald Soprano* and *The Chairs*

[7]

of almost thirty years later; though the Theatre of the Absurd, with the Theatre of Cruelty of A'rtaud, who acted for him in 1922, and Breton's Surrealism, were all, for reasons of temperament, worlds distant from Cocteau. A look over his whole work shows us that he was rapid—inverted in that he used words often in their countersense, depending upon nuance and *placement* to disclose their expanded meaning, which at points makes him very nearly and perhaps actually untranslatable. Devoid of connective tissue, which in Cocteau, although he grasped the idea of particularism more than fifty years ago, was probably the consequence of a humility which withheld him from the implied omniscience even of stitching up a narrative. Deft; which he used and abused. He probably thought Nijinsky rising from a blue pool in "fabulous India" *(The Blue God)* clever indeed, but the trickery of effects was soon to be a double-entendre because, in the gathering climate of realism, it made the manipulator faintly ridiculous. And suspect.

On a spring night in 1913, Stravinsky broke the mold. Nijinsky, Cocteau witnesses, could not understand why the audience hissed and catcalled *Le Sacre du Printemps* when it had applauded *Le Spectre de la Rose*. But Nijinsky was not bright, except in his limbs, and Cocteau was very much so. That night, after the première of scandal, riding in a fiacre with Diaghilev, Stravinsky, and Nijinsky, he got the idea for *Parade*.

Three hucksters cajole the crowd in front of a circus tent, insisting that the parade is not the show and urging them to go in. Nobody does. They collapse into a heap one upon another. The performers insist that the show is within not without and that the crowd should go in. No one does.

A small germ of the Theatre of the Absurd might be discoverable here, we might think, if we did not learn the untold story of what lay behind the Cubist ballet. Cocteau persuaded the ogre Picasso to attempt the stage décor, horrible heresy in the eyes of Stalinian Cubism, which Picasso shrugged off indifferent-ly enough; in consequence Cocteau enjoyed the humiliation (the word choice is probably quite correct) of seeing nearly all his ideas displaced in rehearsal, in a cellar in Rome, by the spontaneous ideas of Picasso. It seems that Cocteau did keep the "little American girl," a figure he had for some reason turned over in his mind for years, but mainly the show stemmed outward from the stage set instead of the reverse.

The impact of Picasso, thus commenced in 1916, has an import infinitely beyond that of *Parade* itself, finally produced May 18, 1917, in Paris in a scene of scandal, from which "Apollinaire saved Picasso and me because he was in uniform and that was the time of the war." Cocteau knew Stravinsky first, and it is quite probable that the idea of a *succès de scandale* by outraging the bourgeoise did come to him initially from Stravinsky, but Stravinsky had a cold rectitude and Cocteau was saturated (discreditably, he considered) with rectitude, if very much of his particular type. The two quarreled, made it up, which would mean as always that Cocteau had run to him penitently but sincerely in supplication, and that Stravinsky had known not to miss an opportunity, as Cocteau did too, and the two collaborated during 1926 on an "oratorio" which emerged as *Oedipus-Rex* in May, 1927, directed by Stravinsky. The derivation of this work merits a parenthesis, because it bears on something repetitive and unnoticed.

As we sink into Cocteau's climate, we discern that the disapproval of him (quite unintelligent and misconstruing as to the surface of the thing often enough) must have been somehow sought, called as the knife is said to be by some magnetism in the breast of the victim in certain murders. But while this was unmistakable in his atmosphere we will be very wrong to see him unilaterally as a *martyr imaginaire.* His life had paradox imbedded in its structure. When he was world-famous and said

[9]

to be the leading man-of-letters of France, he had great trouble in getting published and staged. A not isolated case in point is *Oedipus*. He wrote it in 1922; it was set to music and staged by Stravinsky in 1927; it was produced, as *Oedipe-Roi*, only in 1937. A young actor named Jean Marais had a very small role in the cast.

Picasso had of course bowled over less permeable individuals than Cocteau but for Cocteau he had a meaning so disruptive, so cumulative, that we might with confidence place the inception of Cocteau's career in the 1916–18 years. Some critics have insistently associated him with the school of destruction, but we may feel this is as though to confuse D. H. Lawrence with the gamekeeper. Cocteau in the *Ode to Picasso* (1919), and in the eulogistic and very penetrating study *Picasso* (1923), would take us on a tour of the cave of the Minotaur and then rather hopefully suggesting there is after all a monster in *every* cave imply: "For instance, mine. Here is the thread." It wasn't very convincing. Three individuals moved him more deeply than anybody else—they were Picasso, Dargelos, and Radiguet—and they all did so by the same quality: heartlessness. A sort of arrogant, careless indifference. A disregardful egotism. Dargelos was the cockerel of the college, both in Cocteau's best-known book and film and in real life at the Lycée Condorcet. I have been with Picasso when a blue French telegram signed "Ton, Jean" arrived and seen the amused smile that passed from Picasso to Jacqueline, then the blue bit of paper supplicating a visit flutter as it was tossed aside into a wastebasket.

Examination of the body of Cocteau's work shows us that his rather sweet-toned mockery is always directed upon himself; whereby he is shut forever from the mockers of others, such as the Dadaists, the Surrealists, the eventual Theatre of the Absurd. Yet the result is that he is made subtler than those he emulated as well as he could. He understood Picasso well, or else he could not have been the best explicator of him of the hundreds. But the Picasso he devises has an odd personal inflection. He is the man of *désinvolture*, a kind of easy unconcern, the pure male principle, but he is at the same time impenetrable. It is easy to see why Cocteau should have envied this; at the same time the elaboration he gives his fatal type is decisive. These men offer the terrible temptation to break open the shell and make them feel what you feel for once.

There is a cross-stitching throughout Cocteau's work which obliges us to sort it, as he did not, for our own clear-seeing. Ballets, sketches, skits, monologues tumble forth at various times over forty years; fourteen of them are collected in *Théâtre de Poche* (Pocket Theatre) published in 1955. A few tell us something. In *Le Boeuf sur le Toit* (1920) the barman wears a head of Antinoüs. A head of Antinoüs, the emperor Hadrian's ephebe, was the only thing Cocteau kept, but kept all his life, of the effects of his grandfather, the redoubtable Eugène. *Le Pauvre Matelot*, set to music by Darius Milhaud as many of Cocteau's things were, is one of only two in an *œuvre* of nearly exactly one hundred compositions, about three-quarters of which were fictions of one sort or another, that is a "good story" in the Maupassant sense. The second, which its author characterized with one of his double-edged remarks as his worst play "but therefore naturally one of my most popular," will merit our full-length examination for the peculiar light it throws on Cocteau in particular and in general on the Rimbaud-derived school of creators who listen to "the other" *(l'Autre)*. Cocteau, we conclude, had all the attributes of the popular writer of the *pièce de boulevard* except shamelessness at success—his desire to please stands to our examination perhaps as the principal motive of his life, black-starred in that it led a hostile, or shallow, or, in journalism, column-inch-seeking criticism to characterize him as a mere sycophant, with a monotony that turned allegation

[11]

into fact (a fact is what people think is true), but his desire to please did not extend to pleasing a theatregoing public. We shall see how dangerously near he verged at times; what exculpation he proferred, singly here sham because he had here to conceal a crime alongside which homosexuality, etc., paled. Had he lived in another age than ours we feel he would, following the true bent of his gift, owed to a brain rapid as had perhaps not existed in France since Voltaire (he loathed the comparison, and it was true), have been little more than a twicefold superior Noel Coward. Participating at what may be the last supper with all of us, this, at least, was beyond his reach. It must have pained him to displease, even the bourgeosie. Revile the bourgeois he did, in the best twentieth-century convention; he went beyond this and into *terra* (then little after 1918) *incognita,* anticipating an art movement not yet come, but probably our future.

In *Les Mariés de la Tour Eiffel* (sometimes translated as The Eiffel Tower Wedding Party, a title for once better than that of the original, for usually he is traduced by his translators as though they do not really understand him) his craft a first time surfaces. Craft finally came to serve him in a very Cocteauan way: it provided "obstacle," that is dexterity had to be overcome.

Every prolific professional's work must overlap but Cocteau's did in a quite original way: that of transferring bons mots, aphorisms from his fictions to subsequent life, putting them sometimes into his mouth, sometimes that of somebody else (one of his Names cramming the twenty volumes of his *Poésie Critique*), or perhaps at different places in the critique the same remark, now given another, now given himself, as if disdaining history—in the interests of a spirited telling—or intending to baffle, intrigue, tickle, or plague our literalness, provided we notice.

In 1923, two years before his first full-length play, he published his first novel, *Le Grand Ecart,* though he claimed he had

[12]

written most of *Le Potomak*, published the following year, a decade earlier, thus putting it exactly amid the destroyed fin-de-siècle poetical works. While we find all Cocteau's work subliminally autobiographical, often revealing most when it seeks to conceal, in *Le Grand Ecart* he is autobiographical in a sense that in the rest of his work he is not—that is, in the sense of Hemingway's *The Sun Also Rises*. It can be read as a report of events then current—not transmuted by imagination. We will want to return to it for what it yields about Jacques Forestier-Cocteau, even to the way he carefully cultivated his hair into the uncontrollable chanticleer bush; here we sufficiently note that while Stopwell, incarnation of the egregious Dargelos this time under another name, is clearly the admired character and carrier of the grail of holy *désinvolture*, Jean Cocteau (Forestier) loves a *girl*. He did; and her name was Adèle Martin, though she called herself Madeleine Carlier for the cabarets where she danced. Later she became a dancer with Mistinguett. He took her to the ultimate moment before he "found out" and then, textually, withdrew like a knife from the wound.

I found this so surprising that I asked him if it were true. "Exact," he said.

The novel is thus all too correctly *Le Grand Ecart* (the split, not *The Big Split* as translated, for in French *écart* means deviation and *grand écart* means split, as "the splits" on stage—this is not a picayune distinction because we shall see that it carries us directly to the heart of Cocteau's method, and the naked "split" is, by its starkness, far more final than the amplification). To have gone even to penetration was not bad for a man who would live with his mother till forty, and the unquestioned fact that somewhere along the route to this ordinarily desired destination he did not tumble that it was not for him seems a well-nigh incredible instance of his very real innocence. (I shall differentiate throughout this essay between facts I know

[13]

to be true and "poetic" facts of Cocteau's invention true to him perhaps in a psychological way.)

His final short works—1940 to 1960—were monologues, two of them for Edith Piaf, whose death, announced on October 11, 1963, is said to have provoked his later the same day (which it did; but not in the manner known)—one which, written in a single night, provided her with her first dramatic stage role.

Most important of the monologues is not in the Pocket Theatre. It was for a time in the *Théâtre Complet;* but is not in the two-volume Gallimard, which we may take for definitive. *The Human Voice* engages us at various levels. Like the others, it betrays a verve hardly found elsewhere save in some of the monologues of Chekhov. Cocteau never honed, and, famous for it though he was, the *mot juste* was the ultimate horror (which he constantly achieved). If he alternated effort and flair, sometimes bewilderingly, though he tells us that throughout the whole body of his work he could pick out every sentence written by "Cocteau" (by which he meant naturally) and every word forced, nevertheless he would never have pruned to excellence by removal, the Hemingway method, far less for correctness, for that way, he said, we pluck the thorn from the thing, take away its sting. His extensive writing on writing shows us. He despised Flaubert. *The Human Voice* (1930) marks the insertion of painstaking errors in French, platitudes, redundancies.

A woman (jilted) talks on the telephone. That's all. Recorded eventually by Simone Signoret, filmed in 1947 by Rossellini two years after the shattering success of *Rome, Open City,* the play had a diffusion (he was fifty-eight that year) Cocteau seldom enjoyed until at the end of his life. But this isn't what really interests us. The stage production marked the entrance of the avant-garde playwright into the confines of the Comédie-Française—with precisely the same deliciously unconvincing, perhaps secretly intentionally so, argument he would use on entering the French Academy a quarter century later in 1955:

[14]

that the most revolutionary act possible to a revolutionary was to enter the Establishment. Of the Academy he said with a woebegone expression: "They have imposed it on me. It would be discourteous not to accede." We know that entry to the French Academy is upon successful petition of the candidate, after a careful solicitation of his Academician friends. From 1930, in fact from a decade before this, we are going to have to look at a different Cocteau—the anticonformist conformist.

The Eiffel Tower Wedding Party (1921) is distinguished by the rapid, metallic, dehumanized recitative of the phonographs, which carries the whole burden of the dialogue except for two brief lines spoken almost at the end by the birdie camera—who wants to rendre the general engulfed earlier in the action, a pun as rendre means both to give back and to vomit up, a premonitory hint of word-deftness finally to reach uncanny heights of velocity, depths of profundity that were perhaps born of the verb and not thought. Clearly, by the dry, uninflected, machinal tone we are thrust forward to the Assimil-record dialogues of Ionesco. And probably, we may surmise, in part for the same reason—après-guerre. But whatever the full case with the Absurdists may be, with Cocteau there is another element he may or may not have been aware of at the time (manifold are the origins of things)—it was the correspondence of this phonosound with a tonality native to his own pitch, which he could by emphasis assume with his own voice. The birth of an aspect of his style was in this, and it would be dangerous to assign what to which. At any rate, we find him as early as Antigone late in the following year talking out very rapidly and high through a peephole in the backdrop as the choir "as if reading aloud from a newspaper"—parodying revival of the Greek in that we are shown not that antiquity is but that it no longer can be—then ultimately as The Voice: La Machine Infernale (1934), his play probably most likely to endure. Late in life he instructs himself

[15]

in a recording studio: "Read your poems as much like a machine as possible; as little humanly as possible."

We are shown the first level of the Eiffel Tower. The stage is empty. Phono 2 remarks the sight of an ostrich crossing the stage. The stage remains empty. Phono describes the stalking of the ostrich by a hunter. The stage remains empty. Phono observes him fire: he kills a telegram. A real telegram flutters down from the flies. The wedding party assembled, a wedding photo is to be taken. Instead of the birdie, a baby pops out of the camera. It is the portrait of the wedding. It sets itself at once to assassinate its parents, the bridal couple. As if he were writing today, Cocteau has the baby explain itself with the shriek (uttered turn on turn by both Phonos): "I want to live my life!"

Criticism of course attributes this sort of thing to Jarry, which would make Cocteau a sort of precursor at mid-station. He was aware of Jarry—he said to Picabia, the overrated Dadaist painter, that he deplored playwrights dull and forgotten such as Jarry and Ibsen—but he didn't meet him. Had he, he would have told us so a thousand times over; doubtless human sympathy would have altered his reading of *Ubu.*

It is odd when you think of it to attribute the whole of Absurdity in a world not unabsurd to a puppet play for children—written by one Charles Morin and made into its present form by his schoolmate at the Lycée de Rennes, Jarry, when the latter was fifteen. Passing note might be given to the peculiarity that these seminal works having absurdity (want of grown-up logic) were in fact written by children (Lautréamont barely out of his teens at the publication of *Maldoror*) or else in the marvelous case of Dodgson told to a girl-child by one who had a perhaps too great penchant for creatures of that sort (eternally carrying around large safety pins in his pocket in case there should be a a little girl who needed her frock pinned up!) and so would be peculiarly susceptible to her imaginary world at sacrifice of his own. Cocteau had something in common with Dodgson; with

[16]

the purveyors of the demon of the absurd, very little. He was not cruel, and his angels were of another sort.

In 1918 he met Radiguet. If his abasement before Picasso seems to us clearly sexual—which he fortified by naming Picasso a duo, both male and female, thereby perhaps declaring wishful aspiration or reaching some affinity that would hearten him—still his submission to Radiguet, who was half his age when they met, Radiguet fifteen, Cocteau thirty, seems to require a less open-and-shut explanation. Radiguet died at twenty in 1923. Hence we have conjecture and Cocteau's often mythomaniacal word to go on. He tells us that Radiguet's second novel, *Le Bal du Comte d'Orgel*, the boy did not even write but dictated "smoothly and without hesitations" to Georges Auric. The depth of his love for Radiguet is unquestioned. It drenches *Opium* (1930) where he tells us quite simply that in taking to opium his intent was not to dull his grief at Radiguet's death, as said, but to destroy himself. However, his body resisted the drug and he could never get to a strong enough dose before accommodation caught him up.

Did he attempt to rear a monument to Radiguet—or, better said, make a monument of Radiguet? He laid to Radiguet— out of love, out of a self-effacing benignity almost self-mortifying?—his fundamental note, the fundamental Cocteauan originality—which bids fair to be the tone of the time when the shaggy revolutionaries shall have worn our appreciation out. Conformity is revolt when revolt is secure in the chair; classic form is essential or you will not have the mold of it to break. Cocteau or Radiguet? In fact one feels that had Radiguet not arrived he would have invented him.

Cocteau had, like everyone in the tailwind of romanticism, to be individual; but he didn't like this. His brilliancy embarrassed him, he was not arrogant, therein and not in questions of the inward and automatic source of writing lay the basis of his famous quarrel with André Breton, one of the few sincerely angry

[17]

quarrels of his life, for he found it nearly impossible to dislike anyone—in this and in Breton's obviousness. Cocteau scribbled on envelopes, even the sides of his tennis shoes in one case, and never used a desk but rather wrote on his knees, in his own attempt to achieve "automatic" writing—release the demon of the unconscious or the verb, whichever it really was, by shutting the paralysis of the mind—but he would never have turned it into a system, for to his swifter intellect that contravened its very meaning. In sum, if one could be more *révolté* than the revolt, newer than the now somewhat dated new, leave the obtuse behind, if reluctantly also leave behind the genuine destroyers, such as Picasso, at the same time by so doing regain the world of Ingres and Diderot . . . ?

We isolate, at the least, a temperamental affinity.

Whether this instigated his turn at this time, 1918–21, to adaptation of the classics or not, it probably has something to do with his extreme success, for as passage of time peels merely passing appearances off it is seen that in the *pseudo* Greek— the word should be emphasized—Cocteau finds his métier, not all at once and never satisfactorily as to stagecraft, of which he had too insistently much. Yet if his stage maneuver is obvious and distracting by being too present, in the meaning of his adaptations he is subtle, complex, velvety in a way that makes the blunter practitioners of neo-Greek such as Sartre and Camus fall out of the mind, the immediacy of their moment once past. They know plainly what they are about, we feel, and shortly lose interest. What Cocteau is about, however, we find different, and increasingly so degree by degree. The gods bilked Oedipus, he tells us, for they *gave* him the answer to the riddle of the Sphinx . . . being gods, as gods were understood then in Greece, they would have, if they had not wanted him to guess it, withheld it from his mind. They *betray* him into superconfidence whereby he goes on to fornicate with his mother. Orpheus perhaps does not turn toward his wife out of egotism of any sort;

[18]

but is perhaps prey of the Bacchantes, for he has created misogynous and perhaps homosexual rites. Cocteau has not forgotten that that was a world in which men were to the gods as flies are to little boys, and he does not modernize its mind, though he does its surface. It is this broth, into which he does not hesitate to stir his profoundest personal preoccupations, that progressively is thick with ambiguity.

Taken as chronology of his development or his spirit, the novels are anterior to his theatre. In fact, all but one were published before his real emergence on stage in April, 1934.

His most—his only—widely-read novel has had a distinguished translator. Rosamond Lehmann has given *Les Enfants Terribles* a flow, a thickness; whereas the original is made up of a series of simple, direct poetic statements. It is hard to say if it should have been made sound English or not, but it does seem odd to read a tone so untrue to Paris, so true to London. My inscribed copy of Miss Lehmann's translation says . . . *à toi ce portrait de mon livre. Jean.* That's about it. Yet Cocteau himself, as has been observed earlier, made "portraits" of novels, even movies, fashionable boulevard plays. By this he meant to suggest he did not make these things, but only seemed to. Sometimes— particularly in one or two of the plays—this is thin. What is the difference between a portrait of a *pièce de boulevard* and a *pièce de boulevard?* Nothing; if the portrait be accurate. It would be unfair not to add that Cocteau's translation of Jerome Kilty's *Dear Liar*, about George Bernard Shaw, gives us a most Cocteauan Shavian. When he translated *A Streetcar Named Desire* he worked from a word-for-word translation, then, cued in, simply wrote the play in French. The *scintillant* is what is missing in translations of Cocteau's work; the inchoate.

Les Enfants Terribles was written at the Saint-Cloud clinic where, in 1928–29, he was recuperating from a cure for addiction to opium. I remember the pathos of his joy when the novel

[19]

came out in paperback, he then France's most famous literary figure throughout the world, and he was at last on the wire-rack stands outside the drugstores with Françoise Sagan.

Paul and Elisabeth, brother and sister, live in *vase clos*—that is, the hothouse element of their own conceptions, a non-incestuous incestuous common bedroom into which Dargelos breaks, by striking Paul with the snowball at the Lycée Condorcet play site, later by sending the ball (black globule) of poison which provokes Paul's suicide.

The incident is a personal symbol. The following year the same catalyzing incident of Dargelos and snowball appears in *The Blood of a Poet*—his famous, and first, film. Pierre Dargelos was a real boy at school with Cocteau at the Lycée Condorcet. Dargelos may be taken for the figure of breaker of the isolation within self-preoccupation of a vase of glass, rather than Michael, who would marry Elisabeth, or Agathe, who would marry Paul, advanced as intruders by the intrigue.

Gerard loves Paul. Paul loves Dargelos in the peculiar sense of worshiping his image—even his principle, if this is not hindsight. Dargelos cracks Paul upon the chest with a snowball—"like a fist of marble"—in which he has or has not, it is never clarified, rolled up a stone. Paul succumbs in a most surprising way. Carried home to "the room" by Gerard, he in effect never comes out again. He founders; the blow has been in delayed action (the time of opium dream as Cocteau describes it) mortal.

Circumstantially—the event-structure of the whole book, if you exclude this first one of pelt by Dargelos and its sequel, seems curiously at one side, as though it hardly mattered—Dargelos is expelled . . . for casting pepper into the preceptor's face next day when called to account. Paul has no further incentive to return to school, his education ceases.

Gerard transfers his affections from Paul to Elisabeth (he is now living with them in the room some of the time, shortly all the time). Elisabeth becomes a fashion mannequin. Thus she

[20]

meets Agathe, a fashion model after a tenebrous life following the suicide of her parents, which climaxed their addiction to drugs. She too soon moves in.

We are probably not asked to swallow literally a foursome advancing from seventeen to twenty mingling their sexes in one room, without overt consequence. Half a dozen years earlier in *Le Grand Ecart* Cocteau had given us a sexual atmosphere like that of our own time — when Jacques Forestier finds his girl friend in bed with another girl, she remarks, almost with indifference, "Would you rather I betrayed you with a man?" In the present context, Gerard present as if the role of spectator needed to be filled, Paul parades about naked in the room while his sister watches him with the severity of a Greek Muse. We are meant to sense a climate. Little wonder the grain is of sadistic teasing, which repeatedly explodes into outrage.

Suddenly, Agathe is seen to resemble Dargelos. And at this, something remarkable happens. All the cut-outs of movie stars, murderers, boxers, Paul's gallery pinned around the walls, are seen equally to resemble Dargelos. Paul tyrannizes over Agathe; she resembles Dargelos and, a rather abject creature, has fallen in love with him.

One reason for the peculiar asexual sexuality may be that Cocteau has set the calendar back. Significantly, Dargelos is the only character in the book described physically. A photograph exists of Dargelos. He is as Cocteau shows him, and a fox-like little Jean Cocteau looks out of the same group photo, but these times at the Lycée Condorcet were in the early and not the late teens. Which may explain grimacing, stickings-out of tongue, and so forth, which seem to belong to a younger age than is assigned, and the deviation of evident sexuality into verbalism.

Nonetheless, Michael, "an American Jew" — he gets hardly further shrift than this — is brought in. He does deflower the *sacré* virgin Elisabeth, we are informed in a single sentence

[21]

negligently, the only one of its kind that goes into carnal detail in the book. It is instructive to see what happens to him. On the eve of marrying Elisabeth (which he has somehow already legally done), Michael goes off to the Riviera for a week. He is decapitated by his scarf trailing from his open sports car. Writing this in 1929, Cocteau would have known this would make everyone think of Isadora Duncan's death in the same extraordinary way only two years earlier.

It is significant perhaps of something in the mind of Cocteau that, superb in imagination, highly inventive as to trickery, stage and film device, and form, he exhibits a startling paucity of narrative invention—most startling perhaps in that he employs it, lets it pass his censor. *La Machine Infernale,* probably his profoundest play, is marred by an opening so plainly reproducing the ghost scene and soldiers on the rampart in *Hamlet* that we are left with the question: how could he have permitted such a distraction? . . . he would have known he would make us think of the best-known play in the world. (But see final paragraphs.) Such gaucherie is kin with his introduction of "Cocteau" by name into more than one play—awkwardness of which he himself was so much aware that he sometimes provided footnote instructions for the stage director who wished to take it out. It is too much to say this is mad egotism, as it might be in Bernard Shaw; more probably it had something to do with his conviction that the clumsy was desirable in art—"I should be crushed if I were told that I had grace," he told me. He had it. There is, everywhere in Cocteau, a tendency to *disrupt.*

Left Michael's house and fortune through Elisabeth, the ménage moves, but does not change. Gratuitously, Dargelos provides a bullet of poison (through Gerard). Paul kills himself, agonizing at length. Elisabeth, toward the end of this, shoots herself.

We are told that the novel addressed itself to half a dozen people, that the author had no idea hundreds upon hundreds of

[22]

young people lived just such a life, and that the book eventually created its world of imitators—whereby everything was falsified "because you do not live strangely unless you are unaware of it." The *cipher* of Cocteau language is to come; on the other hand we have here the *nudity*. His style is bare. It is a manner for highlighting. The tyrannizing of Dargelos in the person of Agathe, for instance, is let stand out clotted by neither narrative nor verb. It is, therefore, stark. It is what he had to tell us: the room, Dargelos: the rest is, except as novelizing used to be seen, of no great matter.

He has often, therefore, particularly in France, been named precursor, or actually originator, of the antinovel: the swing which will end in Robbe-Grillet, for instance, describing in detail the furniture of a room rather than the people in it. But Robbe-Grillet is attempting to show the nonhumanity of an age, as Cocteau did too, with pretty well everyone else understandably, but not here. He *had* written a novel which is distinctly avant-garde in the most evil sense, *Le Potomak*, which he aptly characterized in a preface written supposedly in 1916 to the text written supposedly 1913–14 as, he then having met Gertrude Stein whom he was the first European author to celebrate, a prologue to a prologue to a prologue. *Le Potomak* was not published till 1924, therefore the conjecture about actual as against announced dates of the contents, for Cocteau was a retoucher and remaker of history to its perfection. But the artificer had genius in his fingertips (where the writing instrument is held) and he did not go on to the utter disintegration of the brain which modern novel-writing implies, but shifted to the stage where there is at least the vise of the proscenium. In *Les Enfants Terribles* he itemizes the room justly, not because things have overrun people in the general world but rather because the room dominates.

Le Potomak does not keep to focus; it is a confetti of ideas, maxims, some of which indeed he held to throughout his life.

Le Fin du Potomak, written early in 1939—apocalypse and the destruction of Paris, and so on, very much in the mass tradition, his last novel, he claimed too to be omniscient—pridefully omniscient in that it anticipated the second world war. As did *Le Potomak* by its horror the first. But a close look at Cocteau suggests the possibility that clairvoyance may be the capacity of a preternaturally rapid intelligence to read small hints. Perhaps to be unable not to read them. It was chastening (*chaste* was the word he reserved for the highest quality of style) to be in Cocteau's actual presence offstage. Then the ideas took on a different coloration—shorthand of a mind inept, because too swift, for communication. He seemed to come brunt up against a wall of finality in expression, having got to the conclusion too soon; the epigrams were little jeweled knives he put into himself.

Thomas the Impostor (1923), like *Le Grand Ecart* earlier the same year, is for the most part overt autobiography.

Misia Sert—"Madame de Bormes"—was a well-known art patroness. She really did organize a private ambulance convoy to the front. Cocteau went along. He "loved" the bombardment of Rheims, the noble nude-to-the-waist gunners dug into the dunes near Dunkerque: it is not one of his best moments. Poetic description of real death and real wounds—"to which gangrene added its black musk"—does *not* appeal. The story is of a hoax; but perhaps "visited upon" Thomas. De Fontenoy is a leading general of France: Guillaume Thomas is from (de) Fontenoy. Asked if he is related to the general, because called Thomas de Fontenoy, he acknowledges he is his nephew—and at once *becomes* such. Shot, he must confront the exigency by the rule he has made his. He thinks: "I am lost if I don't pretend to be dead." He dies.

Something we find overlooked in Cocteau is his portrayal of women. He does it not as might be expected but as a genuine man might outraged by their impudence, as for example in the days which shall follow Women's Lib, reminiscent of G. B.

Shaw's remark: "You give them equality in vote, work etcetera and they remain women and you men, and you call that equality?" It is a bit surprising to see Cocteau busy at putting down the insolence of women.

He is, we find, a lightning conductor—he conducts to himself the lightning. Even from the first he is adept at putting himself in the wrong, but then blinded by the keenness of youth he perhaps thought himself brilliant; later it was very different.

There are very many images throughout Cocteau of this sort: what does the canvas think and feel, as it is spat upon, sullied, splattered, abused, in order to become a masterpiece?

In *Le Grand Ecart* (1923) we see Cocteau not as in a mirror darkly but face to face.

I pried from him that he modeled Peter Stopwell on Steerforth in Dickens, because he could not deny he had just before writing *Le Grand Ecart* published an article on Dickens and Steerforth, nor deny the evident fraternity of the rhythm of the names; but he modeled Stopwell on Dargelos just the same.

Jacques Forestier weeps easily; how shall he conceal his heart, which is too big? In *Thomas the Impostor,* Thomas, the truth in falsity because falsely true or truly false, says: "I trick. I am unfortunate: I am adept. How can I get out of it?" Jacques has a suspect elegance; his reputation for "spirituality" comes from nothing but the fact that he thinks too fast; he admires beautiful young bodies, of whichever sex; he can be demoralized by a word; he is thin, nervous, "skinned alive"; this aristocrat who is a member of the people can bear neither the aristocracy nor the people: to appear as unartificial as possible he resorts to artifice, and ten times a day "deserves to be guillotined." Had Jean Cocteau been solely either Jacques or Thomas . . . That he was both brings forth the corrupt beauty of the later phase.

We read a novel with the attractions of 1973 published exactly fifty years earlier: detailed description of taking of drugs; instant sex; lesbianism. True, the drug-taking is a suicide attempt, but so extensively (very unusual in Cocteau) and precisely detailed that we wonder if Cocteau's first meeting with opium was the year after Radiguet's death and publication of this book (not named, the drug here seems to be cocaine). Over this, the "Greek god" (had he not somewhat deformed himself by broad-jumping at which he is champion) Stopwell presides monosyllabically. An Englishman written by a Frenchman, he says next to nothing, except occasionally lets fall a word in praise of Oxford; his plus fours, his pipe, do not conceal his real identity. And toward the end of the book there is an astonishing merging of identities. The merging of Agathe into Dargelos in *Les Enfants Terribles* half a dozen years later is prefigured in a sudden paragraph. Cocteau simply must have tumbled on this, a discovery; an "exhalation." It is so abrupt. Then amplified it later in the subsequent book. Stopwell has taken Germaine from Jacques; suddenly Jacques wonders if he has not mistaken the target of his desire. No, no. Germaine. For she is of the race. "For there is a race on earth of those who never look back, don't suffer, can't love, never fall ill; those diamond-hard who write" (ineffacably) "on the transparent people of glass." Jacques is one of these latter, Petitcopain too; a race fluid, drowned. But a diamond, what is it? Son of coalmen become rich. "Thus Jacques manufactures with words—hogties the demon, puts himself on guard against a danger too well known." This is the true end of the book; and in fact but a page from the brief epilogue which terminates it. The novel's final line: "He [Jacques] realized that to live in the world he should have to follow its modes, and that his heart would not bear it."

Self-revealing at any level—most unadulterated of anything in Cocteau in the description of Forestier—the novel does tamper with fact, both real-life and psychological (Cocteau's first novel, and never again will he so overtly novelize—we are only a year from the "splintered" *Le Potomak,* prologue of his middle period later to be obfuscated). Madeleine Carlier apparently was very much like Germaine, and we should not give Cocteau too much credit as visionary in forepainting the in-a-bed-out-again folkway of our day. Yet, though the skating rink scenes and others are all quite true, he was obliged in the interest of his plot to alter reality both real and psychological, and Jacques, having "withdrawn like a knife from the wound" while Germaine beneath him grimaces like "Desdemona in death throes upon not under the pillow," nevertheless with plotty frequency returns to the trough. Cocteau contorts truth in another way. That Jacques be the lover, he makes Petitcopain (nickname meaning something like "the little friend") his other self: to lick up to Stopwell, be spurned, by a man beautifully cruel, flawless. We are here on the threshold of a presence later to be transvested—Galahad in *The Knights of the Round Table* played by Jean Marais.

A reprimand for certain biographers—perhaps themselves of the persuasion, or hunting sales, who too much emphasize aspects of homosexuality—is contained in the lesson of grave dignity in the comportment of Jean Marais in the last summer of Cocteau's life. They had long since ceased to be lovers, yet with the seriousness of an ex-husband Marais cared for Cocteau after the April heart attack, and there was no jealousy but only gratitude from Edouard Dermit, who himself told me of this. Jean Marais at the grave on October 16, 1963, demonstrated ramifications of a form of love not usually elaborated, and not different from the maturity of any form of love.

Very loose, very condensed—curt—adaptation commenced the adaptations of the classics: *Romeo and Juliet,* written in 1918, but, a persistent difficulty, unstaged till 1924. Confronted with the difficulty of being a born playwright, Cocteau had an interesting occasion. He could do his talent in. Unfortunately,

[27]

straight blow of the snowball wasn't his way—there is a stutter, uncertainty, interesting after all, finally a discreditable way-giving and he writes at least two dramas measurably well-made by any scale, excusing himself as best he can. Before this, he has a great period.

To situate Cocteau, we can hardly do better than employ a metaphor of his. *The Blue Train,* his operetta for the Ballet Russe in 1924, had for curtain what was, repainted, to be one of the great works of Picasso's neoclassic phase—the two mis-shapen, lumpy women running on the beach. (Usually called *Deux Femmes Courant sur une Plage.*) The well-nigh inconceivable effect this one man had on everyone he met and on a whole generation does not concern us here; but we note that he had arrived in neoclassicism by 1924. What, then, was the difficulty? At the Saint-Jean-Cap-Ferrat villa where he spent most of the last eight years of his life, Cocteau kept a photograph upon an end table, spread out flat. It was incomprehensible. Fume or smoke exploded into wavers and blobs; within this were inscrutable, distorted forms. A cylinder of foil placed down in the center of it, it at once became, on the cylinder, intelligibly Rubens' *Crucifixion.* It had been shot by a camera-in-the-round, to which the cylinder was keyed. The photo itself remained impenetrable as ever. The suggestion was that clarifying life you falsified it.

A curious life lived in the villa, which Cocteau might have invented—Mme Francine Weisweiller, beautiful, the heiress, the neurotic woman, gradually doing herself in; Dermit, who played in the last films, reading crime paperbacks till four in the morning while Cocteau slept; the two others bored to death with the talk of "the greatest talker of France," because they had heard it all, but loving him for the real self he tried to deform in the anticonfessional he felt creation was now becoming and which haunted him. The truth was: you could by conforming to an outlook such as camera-in-the-round or camera-in-any-thing-whatever be intelligible, and that was what you could not do.

Antigone was premièred December 20, 1922, décor by Picasso, music by Honegger, costumes by Chanel. In 1927 the play reemerged masked, the actors, forecasting the familiar figures of the Orpheus films, in black tights so that they looked like a family of insects. The dialogue is struck from flint; Sophocles himself is abridged. As in the progression of the novels everything is cut away to the unsuperfluous essentials, here we begin with everything purified, and Cocteau renders with immense justice and beauty. It is a false start, but we see what playwright he would have been in a century which did not discredit excellence. Antigone and Creon stand "nose to nose" and berate one another with lines of dialogue often no more than a sentence long, and everything is adjusted to a centimeter. He has pace, the natural instinct of the man bred for the theatre. Cocteau has smelt his destiny, his nostrils flare; but he stands in what amounts to a silvery pause, not quite yet taking the plunge. Nor will he err later, as here, though he clung to Antigone all his life as his saint, by putting the Creon-Antigone contest on a dictatorship-freedom basis (a stage beyond which his peers, such as Anouilh, did not get), but rather judging it, as would the Athenians, as did Sophocles, in the light of who had the right of it as to the attitude of the gods—why the great Oedipus drama *La Machine Infernale* twelve years later is of the *machine*.

The first straight play then is *Orpheus,* in 1926. Here Cocteau has marshaled a sufficient quantity of error to please anyone. He is on his own now; there is fidelity only to the core of the Orpheus myth, whereas in the chimelike *Antigone* he is faithful, only heightening, paring; and he blunders admirably. There is reason for this. From Cubism onward a painting is not a rendering of something but it is a painting; thus a play is not life through an invisible fourth wall—but a play. Therein incentive to put fly specks on the invisible wall, to make it seen. Full weight must be given to what had happened to Cartesian thought. With the group to which Cocteau pertained, "I think, therefore I am" had become "I think, therefore I lie." We are cast onto the raft of "instinct."

Heurtebise, a personal symbol, derived from a long poem written in unbroken automatism from start to finish, he tells us, and published as *The Angel Heurtebise* the year before—whose name was that of an elevator stop at which the elevator, in which Cocteau was alone, halted "and it was not his floor," Cocteau's guardian angel hereafter recurrent in the works—is here the glazier who repairs the broken windows of the ménage Orpheus-Eurydice. At one moment he is left literally suspended in air—when Orpheus negligently takes from under him the chair on which he is standing taking measurements, and until he un-noticing replaces it. Definitely asked to take notice, we are thrown bodily out of engagement with the play as happening. We are confronted with the spectacle of a real man, an actor, hung in midair, and we ask ourselves how this is possible rather than take note of Orpheus' absentmindedness, with what it has to tell us of a potential in the Eurydice-Orpheus-Heurtebise relationship (not developed actually until twenty-five years later in the film).

We do not like this scene and we probably do right not to like this play. When the trick is explained to us (it is not to the audience which therefore probably continues distracted for several scenes on) we like it even less. Heurtebise has stood up against the flat, he has a lineman's belt under his coverall with a metal eye at the navel, there is a hole in the flat dissembled by wainscoting and through it a stagehand hooks him; a tiny ledge in *trompe-l'oeil* is therefore sufficient to sustain him as the stage-

[30]

hand tugs at him. We don't like this trifling with us. On the other hand, we can't sensibly sustain that the limpid beauty of *Antigone* could be built into a stage attitude now. In fact, in *Antigone* itself the ambiguity is there. We merely don't notice that means and manner are really not synchronized.

But we can't exonerate Cocteau. The talking horse (it taps with a forehoof) spells out the message that Madame Eurydice shall come back from hell . . . *Madame Eurydice reviendra des enfers.* We are shown that the initial letters form a cipher: MERDE, the French word for excrement. This is the same author who, a year after he has sought us (a public) with a play about Jocasta's daughter, really wrongheadedly breaks into such story structure as *Thomas the Impostor* has by naming a quite minor character Coɪ nel Jocaste. Instinct is at work here; but is it about a business we like? *Epater la bourgeoisie* indeed. How could we differ and maintain our self-respect now? But it does feel different when *we* are the bourgeoisie. Yet by the film *Beauty and the Beast* (1946) overadroit stagecraft will arrive at a strange beauty: the bare forearms of a hundred extras all hold out candles into the hall, are candelabra through the wall; an airplane motor and propeller are installed at the corridor head out of camera range: all the candles go out at once—marvelously, they all come alight together at once; they have been extinguished in the same way but now the film has been reversed and they whiff on.

The infant father of the mirror by which access is obtained to the poetic land in *The Blood of a Poet* (1930, released 1932) is onstage, part of the excessive paraphernalia, the surgical gauntlets of the assistants of Death which bizarrely add the tone of the modern operating room, and so forth, as though the whole Cocteauan future is crowding back upon us, and him—in *Orpheus.* It is, we know, a rectangle of water in *The Blood of a Poet,* into which the poet plunges and back out of which he erupts by reversal of the film, the scene which had been taken flat then simply stood on its side, a technique frequent in this film, such as in skewering little girls flylike to ceilings. Here the mirror is simply *trompe-l'oeil* in sidewall. It is the entrance to Hades. Yet the quality of the metaphor is mixed. The line says, "If you look into a mirror all your life you will see Death work in the hive." He might as well have said the skull of the lion of Samson. Something is at work in the illusionist.

The plot itself is simple. Orpheus and Eurydice have spats, something so constant throughout Cocteau plays that we come to think it, however pretexted, merely because he is blazingly good at rapid-fire exchange. Eurydice is carried off to death (Hades) as the myth decrees. Orpheus goes through the mirror after her and fetches her out again. But on the condition that he never look at her. They spat again. He looks at her. She vanishes forever. He excuses himself poorly to Heurtebise by saying she bloody well deserved this, and that he intended it. Orpheus is then done in by the Bacchantes, for being an offensively disrespectful poet (though we may suspect that the idea of the MERDE conceit preceded and caused its plot use rather than the reverse). They throw his head back up onto the balcony; there is a mummery of the decapitated head in a niche. Now it is a *postiche* head, now that of the actor who plays Orpheus, who, kneeling backstage, sticks his head up through a hole into the niche. Thus he can answer when interrogated by the Superintendent of Police and Clerk of the Court—who prefigure the baleful Fascist-like interrogators after the coming war who permit Cocteau to refer to his film as a *film policier*, thus in his sixty-first year for the first time drawing a genuine mass public. Where—to the head—was he born? Maisons-Laffitte. Where does he live? 10 Rue d'Anjou (where Cocteau at that time lived with his mother). What is his name? Coc . . . (spelling) C.O.C.T.E.A.U. It is perhaps not inappropriate that at this moment

[32]

Cocteau's guardian angel (accused of murdering the poet), Heurtebise, vanishes.

The film, 1950, elaborates elements—among others, Heurtebise and Eurydice have an intrigue. Dread machinery is added to meet the increasing hopelessness of the times. Yet we feel this remains essentially cranked-up metaphysics. More truly poetic: *Beauty and the Beast*—infused with tenderness.

Cocteau collaborated on many films in the film years—the forties, as the thirties were the great theatre years. Most starred Jean Marais. In *Les Parents Terribles* (1938) something quite prophetic from the point of view of film was done. Not changing his stage play in any way, he caused the camera to promenade among the players rather than have the players move other than they had done in the theatre. "When you sit in your loge you can escape significances by inattention but when the camera prowls right in among the players you cannot escape and have to go with it."

We want to see him horizontally, suspecting that historical perspective, verticality, will cause us to see him thinking as he did not. He was certainly an Encyclopedist—who likened himself to Rousseau because he was always pursued by the pack of the Encyclopedists. He condemned Gide, justly, for being the architect of his labyrinth, whereby he betrayed the principle of poetry, which is that it is an intangible and thus a lane intriguing because to its end it is impossible ever to come. He said Victor Hugo was a great poet who nonetheless was afraid to get off National 7, the Paris-Nice highway (and he was afraid to get off it himself). Other times he wanted nothing else. He brings to mind a man known in the 1942 years: a Viennese Jew, he was an ideological Nazi.

The protagonists of *The Sacred Monsters* (1940) are the *monstres sacrés* of the Paris theatre—Sarah Bernhardt and de Max brought up to today, we are told. The play has verve, but

[33]

not the verve of *Les Parents Terribles,* which preceded it by two years, which crackles like brush fire. In *The Sacred Monsters,* nonetheless, there is an odd streak of loving in Esther. ESTHER: "I don't know how to hate, Charlotte. I suppose it's a fault. I don't understand hating. I can't. It happens I run toward people with whom I'm at outs calling: 'What a pleasure to see you!' I just don't think." But possibly in trying to open the shell of the matinee idol Florent, make him feel, make him *talk,* she is submitting to the sublime egotism of sacrificing her happiness to her own real attitude, of marching breast-on onto a sword. And Florent goes with the other woman because among actors it is only vanity that lives.

Contradiction of conventional theatre, Cocteau prefaces *The Typewriter* (*La Machine à Ecrire,* 1941), has, too, reached the end of its curve, as conventional theatre did. The play is more interesting than *Les Parents Terribles,* the success of which provoked it, because it fails. In the earlier play son (played by Jean Marais) and father unknowingly have the same mistress, causing the foreseeable comedy of errors, but there is an unexpected turn to tragedy at the end when the mother kills herself. It seems Cocteau was asked to produce a third "portrait" of the ever-popular *pièce de boulevard,* and acceded. The result is interesting, for we see him collide with his real nature. Basing on a real case of typewritten anonymous letters in the newspapers, he starts out well to write a "police play"—he tells us—but shortly *l'autre,* the inward creative force which may well be nothing but the individuality, takes over. The mystery of the letters cannot be unraveled at a literal level, complication is heaped onto complication, nuance onto nuance. The play, Cocteau tells us, went through twelve rewritings (unique in Cocteau)—and emerges a mess. It seems that there is an incompatibility between exterior and interior interests. Given its point of departure, as the play becomes progressively "truer" it becomes progressively less interesting.

The experience chastened him (a favorite word in his vocabulary) into writing *Renaud et Armide* in verse. Produced two years later in 1943, it was the second of the plays of chivalry. The final play, *Bacchus* (1951), reverts, in fact, to the Creon-Antigone confrontation. Hans, a good-looking village idiot, has been made the pagan god of the village festival, much on the lines of the old primitive god-king who will rule and then be killed, but he throws off his mask and emerges as what would now be called a young revolutionary, and shows the people their confidence is abused by the establishments of Church and State alike; to deal with this is sent the rationalist Cardinal Zampi, equally Creon or The Grand Inquisitor. The cardinal has humor, taste, charm, personality, humanity, diplomacy; what has Hans? That he is right perhaps. It is not sure. He says: if we commit a fault God has committed it, being responsible for our acts. He says: if God is unknowable do we know He may not reward evil and punish good? If more modern, this is less beautiful than the defense of Antigone thirty years earlier: "I stand on the unwritten law which cannot be erased." Hans lowers the "proud woman" Christine by bringing her abruptly to the carnal reality. "I'm the fire and you're the ice. It's a good deal; that it smoke, rage, ravage, and when the red fire penetrates the ice, that it spit like a thousand cats!" "You disgust me. You look at me the way a dog looks at meat." "Dog's right. That's me." — The cardinal has him secretly shot by an archer; announces his recantation (unobtained); has him clothed again as Bacchus, and obliges the people — who have turned against the liberator they acclaimed yesterday — to reverence his corpse. "Fall on your knees! I will pray for his soul."

The play midway between *Renaud et Armide* and *Bacchus* is usually translated as *The Eagle Has Two Heads* (1946). Perhaps it should be singled out — with two others — for the special quality it embodies. The eagle is the two-headed eagle of Austria. A young assassin somehow obtains admission to the cloistered queen, six years his senior. Everything is ambiguous, double, as befits a poet—the author is a poet and the assassin is a poet. Based on a historical example, this is no historical drama; Cocteau here achieves false classicism, as he called it. False classicism, which had gestated in his head since the days of Radiguet, was perhaps his temperamental solution—it had to be *false*. (It would be witless to be truly classic now.) How has the assassin persuaded the queen to keep him with her three days, much of the time in her bedchamber?—this not a story of today. She says: You have killed the queen. A queen does not do this kind of thing. Named Stanislas, he calls himself Azrael. This is a name for the angel of death. Yet it is the queen-anarchist who courts her death (murder of the queen); finally provokes it. She is anarchist though queen, the young are always anarchist but she is thirty; and Stanislas, twenty-five, the anarchist, becomes a royalist when he sees how royalty can be made win—and "improved." All is murky, equivocal. Why would the queen salute her soldiers from the window in Amazonian dress? Why does she expose her face bare to sight—veiled since the assassination of her husband on their wedding day? What sexual ambiguities twist like the at-last disturbed bed sheets in the queen's chamber? At the end, the queen is dead at the top of a library staircase, stabbed; Stanislas is dead at the bottom of it, poisoned.

The final film was *Le Testament d'Orphée* (1960). Heurtebise, the guardian angel, has been accused of murdering the poet as long ago as *Orpheus*. We have been taught to look for variant readings: possibly guardian angels do murder their poets in the course of time? Now the poet dies. Enigmatic lines tell us that this poet is Orpheus too. Cocteau plays the role. So much time was lost searching for finance (small in movie terms) that Cocteau asserts he could no longer comprehend the sense of his script, but would film it anyway assuming it had

[36]

made sense when he wrote it. He announced at the time it was his last film. There was, he considered, no longer a public for the kind of films he wanted to make. Films of enchantment.

He thought of himself as a poet. Poetry of Criticism, Poetry of the Novel, Poetry of Theatre—thus he categorized his work. A difficulty of knowing him is that he projects his poetry best against baffles—against resistance. That is to say, nowhere is he more successfully poetic than when the poetic is *in excess;* when he doubles the cape of meaning. He gives neoclassicism, as we have seen, which was far from his private preserve, his own turn—it is *false* classicism. What does this mean? The distinction is approximately that of "portraited" boulevard plays, plaintive excuse applied, say, to *The Sacred Monsters.* He was inept at the falsifying distortion which characterized, for example, Picasso's neoclassicism. Cocteau's classicism, when he brings it off, we deem classical. Therefore in the twentieth century false.

Less and less was his a locked universe in the fatigued late years when he ceased to try to show how unlocked it was. Beauty and beast are no longer in forced harness; here, then, is a born writer confronted with a disintegrating poetic and literary situation.

He died for his goodness. He has been maligned for little short of three-quarters of a century for seeking publicity, which he sought (Radiguet having written a modern classic, *The Devil in the Flesh,* at seventeen and died at twenty I asked Cocteau what he would have then done had he lived—and was surprised at the spontaneous, genuine answer: "Tended to his publicity, I suppose"). Less emphasized is that a great deal of interview-giving was kindness. On October 11, 1963, he was asked for an obituary on his friend Edith Piaf. He complied though he was in no condition to. Later he was called to the phone to give yet

[37]

a further statement. He was in no condition to leave his bed. He went to the hall anyhow. He spoke for a few moments on the phone; fell away from it dead. It was the final heart attack.

The poetry itself presents us with difficulty; not least for being in English inexistent. Such translation as I have seen "improves" him (sets him straight, gives him form) but it is not Cocteau. The first verse retained (we recall he destroyed a first three volumes)—*Le Cap de Bonne-Espérance* (1919)—depends on page placement. He had the model in Apollinaire; he was trying to reproduce the swooping flights of Garros, World War I aviator with whom he flew.

> Mon encre encoche
> et là
>
> et là
>
>   et là
>
> et
> là
>
> dort
> la profonde poésie

I asked him long after why he did that. This kind of thing dates (something of which Cocteau was in horror, saying: "What strange law is it which decrees that only by ignoring your time do you reproduce it?"—a law he very intermittently obeyed, but sometimes obeyed very much). Nonetheless his answer was strong: "Our most serious problem is, when we write to be read, that the reader is the actor. Not all readers are Louis Jouvet." It is true the stanza would not read as it is if it were put on a straight line. Yet in the formal occasions of verse, such as *Renaud et Armide,* we are shown what Alexandrine splendors Cocteau can write. What formal tradition is agreed nowadays, however, for verse?

He is puritan about his poetry; his rectitude showing here, where another age might least expect it, perhaps because precisely here was the area he considered most important. The piano must be played *sec*—that is, without pedal. His poetry consists, he tells us, in this—that it is a decalcomania of the invisible. Modernity did not help; often we feel as if we are crossing a no-man's-land of splintered glass. He is not everywhere consistent; in the brief *Un Ami Dort*, for instance, as he gazes upon his lover asleep, he writes with a discreditable expansion of heart, by his poetic conviction. A simplicity very translatable—not all Cocteau's poetry is untranslatable. The difficulty, however, is that the most translatable is least Cocteauan, and perhaps we should be content with what his poetry enormously gave his not formally poetic work—the twist off the true again and again, the unwarranted, not the least way the Invisible may make itself present.

In 1962 he published *Le Requiem*. His nineteenth volume of verse, it was written in February and March, 1959, on a pad held overhead "as a fly walks on the ceiling" while he was convalescent from an internal hemorrhage. "I am done in; now the Other can live!" Its one hundred fifty-four pages—there are Halts—has neither punctuation nor syntax. "How am I to impose such artificialities on a river of ink?" In a tone now at last simply noble, he ranges over the preoccupations of a lifetime: Christ, Leonardo da Vinci, Nietzsche, the Spanish bullfight—Dargelos the good student, armed with a snowball, who got his money's worth. He prefaces: "Not without melancholy I find myself, despite an apparent abandon, prisoner of a language structure so rigorous that it remains, alas, untranslatable into any language, though we live by universal contact." The epitaph, added in 1961, his final poetry:

> *Pilgrim halt my voyage*
> *From danger to danger*
> *It is fair you look me in the face*
> *After having disfigured me*

If *The Eagle Has Two Heads* is, particularly if not uniquely, the play of ambiguity, *The Knights of the Round Table* (1937) is the play of charm. A magic charm. Curtain rise on Act Two shows us an empty stage. In a moment a chair removes itself from its place at the wall and goes over and places itself before a table on which are chessboard and chess pieces heaped and strewn. In a moment the chess pieces stand themselves up, take their places for a game. Lancelot and a cohort enter. An enormous pace forward in conjuration is marked from the levitated Heurtebise in *Orpheus* a dozen years earlier, for this is the Black Castle or the Castle of Marvels, castle in semi-ruin of Klingsor appropriated from Wagner's *Parsifal* to be rival magician of Merlin, and it is well it be enchanted. Far from being taken from the dreamed reality, that of the play, to the literal reality, that of actors and stage machinery, we are plunged at once in the heart of the former. And in a moment Lancelot seats himself negligently in the opposite chair, somewhat surprised at the presence of chessboard and deployed pieces in a castle he had supposed deserted. He absentmindedly moves a piece. Immediately a piece opposite moves accordingly. What! Then he recognizes his adversary—it is Klingsor who suffers under no edict to be visible. His *sangfroid* aids him (he has cuckolded King Arthur now eighteen years). Abruptly he moves another piece. Up to you.

What we might risk calling transcendence in the imagination does not limit itself here to making thus visible the invisible Klingsor (he never appears) but vaults to a conception truly magical, perhaps unique in theatre, and wholly successful. This is the means by which Ginifer is made appear. The imp Ginifer, whom Klingsor had put away in a bottle. . . . "Imagine a nice boy like me. In a bottle!" . . . but whom Merlin has rescued, thus making him his slave, is also—unpresent—present. The Plautus-like confusion of identities (but each two-in-one) embroiling the play provides chop-and-change, but at an unearthly leap dis-

[40]

appears beyond this and we enter realms that criticism, always unsympathetic to Cocteau, partly his fault, for everlastingly producing "audacities," did not discern. But it was the stuff dreams are made of, and awful conundrums too.

Cocteau claimed he dreamed the play en bloc. Testimony for unconscious memory is present in the confusion of Wagnerian and Arthurian elements. Criticism withheld belief; for example, an ample *Lancelot du Lac* existed in French. If the play was but a waking dream, it is still remarkable—for the way Ginifer is made very concrete, so that we feel we see him, is by habitation turn on turn of the various principals, even finally Galahad-(Parsifal) himself. And thus each is King Arthur or false King Arthur, Guinevere or false Guinevere, outward appearance in no way changing but comportment very much, depending on whether under control of the mischievous Ginifer or not, or through him malevolent Merlin. Cocteau has, at the least, found an extraordinary symbol. But he presses on. *Whether* Ginifer or not. For he exists in inhabiting them. For—"It is a hard lot to be all of them and never yourself." Cocteau is verging close to a journey to the center of the earth of himself. Supposing (he told me it was) the play was at least in essence dream. What is dream structure? The true-and-false locked in one appearance; the difficulty of the inhabitation of many, which means their inhabitation of you, yourself expulsed.

And Cocteau heaps on this already magical device yet more wonderful employment. In Act One Ginifer is largely present (never in the play does he physically appear, of course); in Act Three, Merlin expelled, he is absent. Which is really better—the world of Act One confused with enchantment? the world of Act Three? It is a final grace of the play that the play does not answer, for the answer depends on who are you.

Cocteau employed the ignoble method, in common with Shakespeare, of often deriving a stage character not from insight or "truth" but from the actor who would play the role. Not so

[41]

with Galahad. Here nevertheless commences what will prevail for a decade, and (suggesting a sobriety in male-male friendship) longer: Marais-Cocteau. The Marais-Cocteau relationship lasted exactly ten years. Jean Marais had had a very small role in *Oedipe-Roi* earlier the same year as that of *The Knights of the Round Table*. The Oedipus of the greatest of the neo-Greek dramas, *La Machine Infernale,* three years earlier in 1934, was to play Galahad. Marais hoped to understudy him. Oedipus was called away by a film: Marais replaced him. Some writers perhaps stand alone, like Towers of Pisa; others, an example is Colette, Cocteau's neighbor in the Palais-Royal, can perhaps not be explained without their lovers. From 1938 *(Les Parents Terribles)* to 1947, and, as said, longer, a double force operates: many of the plays and films were written for Jean Marais; under other circumstances they would have been different.

Be outwardly cogent—an excuse is needed for this—inwardly at odds with play-form not life. Was this a solution? Cocteau's fiasco with *La Machine à Ecrire* shows what happens when you try both on the surface.

La Machine Infernale (1934) was staged by Louis Jouvet, all but last perhaps of the great actor-managers of France, the sacred monsters whose disappearance Cocteau considered largely responsible for the decadence of French theatre, for cinema accustomed audiences to actors necessarily young who spoke low and in "natural" tones and, except in pursuits, etc., moved about little, whereas the sacred monsters declaimed out of their bellies in the "bad roles necessary to good plays" (only Racine could write great plays and great roles together, we are told) and mesmerized everyone.

La Machine Infernale is in texture a woodcut compared to the polished intaglio of *The Knights of the Round Table* or *Renaud et Armide.* We are surprised to feel something of the quality, in texture, not of Anouilh or Giraudoux, but a kind of O'Neill rendering. This is left-footed Greek. An angularity, and, most surprising (Cocteau was forty-three at the writing), naïvety. The whole is very effective. The rugged *arrests*. Here he is closer to his canon of the false classic than ever before or since; but false classic in the common, not final Cocteauan, sense. He keeps to the myth-structure, to Attic outlook before Euripides began to humanize it—we are going to see, The Voice tells us at the outset, the ironic perfection of a machine for catching men to the hilarity of the gods. The *Greek* tragic—for however far he run, boast as he will in the magnificent fullness of resplendent youth, man (oedipus) is done before begun. The play reads less well than *The Eagle Has Two Heads* or *Renaud et Armide*, which we turn to with relief from our daily fare—of oatmeal and malice—as the cycle has come around again, or is coming around, but *La Machine Infernale* plays better. Against the Greek sound, with a friction that chafes, Cocteau runs an inverted drama; devoid of specific trappings to make it modern, thus multidimensional and sardonic comment upon itself as play and life, it is nonetheless in its tonality modern, therein the incongruity. Probably nobody ever speaking classically in homely situations, but improved and refined over the millennia upon which no living man has prise, here The Sphinx, who is merely a young woman like another, speaks nobly—an immediate total change—only when she assumes the socle of Sphinx and slips her naïve seventeen-year-old hands into the griffon-claw gauntlets—and thence until she descends again, when she is again merely a helpless young woman in love with Oedipus, girl-in-love Anubis has trouble keeping to her business. The business to which she must be kept is that of terrifying, of slaughtering the evil and the just alike. But she doesn't much like it.

Four acts constitute the play: The Ghost; Oedipus and the Sphinx; Honeymoon Night (Oedipus and his mother Jocasta); King Oedipus.

The plot is that of the myth: at the birth in Thebes of a son to King Laius and Queen Jocasta an oracle says the son will murder his father and marry his mother. Accordingly, the infant is exposed on a mountain, but a shepherd, finding him, takes him to the king and queen of Corinth, who, childless, cause him to be thought their son. Grown, frightened by oracles saying he will kill his father and marry his mother, Oedipus quits Corinth. At a crossroads, he kills an old man (Laius). He need not be concerned at the removal of this man from the richness of life because in fact it was not his fault, and he puts it out of his mind. Pest and misfortune investing Thebes, these are laid to The Sphinx, and Jocasta announces she will give her hand and co-royalty to him who by killing The Sphinx will free Thebes. Oedipus kills The Sphinx; in consequence marries his mother.

They have two daughters and two sons during seventeen years of incest. The gods now maneuver the machine. The King of Corinth dies; hearing this Oedipus is unseemly joyous at the death of a parent. The oracle has been confounded. But the messenger conveys that on his deathbed King Polybus confessed that Oedipus was not son in Corinth. The shepherd comes forward. The victim of the crossroads is identified. Jocasta hangs herself. Oedipus puts out his eyes with her brooch.

In the first of acts which are in reality set pieces fixing on us not so much a sense of development as of portentous parallelism as the movements hang heavy and contrapuntal, scarf strangulation, brooch fatality, incest in Jocasta's fascination with the young soldier are called up. Tiresias treads on the end of her scarf: "This scarf will strangle me," she says, loosening it irritatedly from her throat. She must actually touch the fat biceps of the soldier coincidentally nineteen, age of her son were he alive. He has the thighs of "a good horse." To her, though she speaks of a son who would be nineteen were he not dead, Cocteau gives an age of "twenty-nine or thirty, thereabouts"—

[44]

generously connubial. They are on a battlement, night, Thebes
rotten and dancing below, ghosts walking: these peculiar echo
touches project a contrapuntal strangeness.

For Act Two we are slotted backward to the same notch in
time. While on the rampart the ghost of Laius is trying to warn
of what is coming but of necessity failing, Oedipus and Sphinx
meet on an empty place on the approaches to Thebes. She is
logical with him. She says (she is seventeen: we recall he is nineteen) that if he would be sure of avoiding the oracle he need
but marry a girl younger than he. Such could not be his mother.
There is a great wistfulness in her desire to cease being a mur-
derous goddess and become but a young girl. A hopeless hope.
But her unarguable point is lost on Oedipus. He is young, hot,
self-sure, full of inexperience and thus certain of the verities:
his real desire is to become King of Thebes. Entailing her death
—she must die if he succeeds—the poor girl gives him answer
and riddle alike. The riddle peculiarly vibrates in nontime, or
the time of the gods, for it touches the familiarity of Shakespeare's seven ages of man, long hence, or back. She is slow
about dying, not liking it much. His preoccupation is: what
manner of carrying her corpse into Thebes will be most striking—dangled under his arm like a soft, collapsed doe; flung over
his shoulder like the lion as borne by Hercules?

We are now on our way to that next most thrilling bed of the
world; less vibrant couch only than that of father-daughter, the
bed of mother-son. Act Three is a tribute to incest. As Oedipus
and Jocasta are on the bed his head by chance lolls against a
cradle—_his_—kept nineteen years by the bed in memory, and
Jocasta, not knowing why, is shot through with wild emotion.
And we are moved in the lurid depths where we once all, in-
dividually and ancestrally, were incestuous. Jocasta consults
herself in the mirror wondering is she still young—so long that
Oedipus behind her tumbles off into sleep. She pulls with

[45]

pressed forefingers at the skin around her cheeks. Is the skin tight?

The last act is brief. The catch has been touched; it but remains that the mortals find their every expectation reversed and crushed. And the gods laugh. Yet it is curiously troubling that little Antigone should appear at the end, begging to go with her blinded father because she does not want to be left with Uncle Creon. Notes sound and cross-sound across distances.

SELECTED BIBLIOGRAPHY

Principal Works of Jean Cocteau

Theatre

Théâtre. Paris, Gallimard, 1948. Vol. I: Antigone; Les Mariés de la Tour Eiffel; Les Chevaliers de la Table Ronde; Les Parents Terribles. Vol. II: Les Monstres Sacrés; La Machine à Ecrire; Renaud et Armide; L'Aigle à Deux Têtes.

Théâtre de Poche. Monaco, Editions du Rocher, 1955.

Orphée. Paris, Stock, 1927.

La Machine Infernale. Paris, Grasset, 1934.

Bacchus. Paris, Gallimard, 1952.

Five Plays. New York, Hill and Wang, 1961. (Orphée; Antigone; Intimate Relations; The Holy Terrors; The Eagle with Two Heads.)

The Infernal Machine, and Other Plays. New York, New Directions, 1963. (The Infernal Machine; Orpheus; Bacchus; The Eiffel Tower Wedding Party; The Knights of the Round Table; The Speaker's Text of Oedipus Rex.)

Criticism

Le Rappel à l'Ordre. Paris, Stock, 1926.

Opium. Paris, Stock, 1930. (Opium. Tr. Margaret Crosland and Sinclair Road. New York, Grove Press, 1958.)

Essai de Critique Indirecte. Paris, Grasset, 1932.

Portraits-Souvenir. Paris, Grasset, 1935. (Paris Album, 1900–1914. Tr. Margaret Crosland. London, W. H. Allen, 1956.)

Journal d'un Inconnu. Paris, Grasset, 1953. (The Hand of a Stranger. Tr. Alec Brown. New York, Horizon Press, 1956.)

La Corrida du Premier Mai. Paris, Grasset, 1957.

La Difficulté d'Être. Monaco, Editions du Rocher, 1957. (The Difficulty of Being. Tr. Elizabeth Sprigge. New York, Coward-McCann, 1967.)

Novels

Le Grand Ecart. Paris, Stock, 1923. (The Miscreant. Tr. Dorothy Williams. London, P. Owen, 1958.)

Thomas l'Imposteur. Paris, Gallimard, 1923. (The Imposter. Tr. Dorothy Williams. New York, Noonday, 1957.)

Le Potomak. Paris, Stock, 1924.

Les Enfants Terribles. Paris, Grasset, 1929. (The Holy Terrors. Tr. Rosamond Lehmann. New York, New Directions, 1957.)

Le Fin du Potomak. Paris, Gallimard, 1940.

Poetry

L'Ange Heurtebise. Paris, Stock, 1925.
Le Cap de Bonne-Espérance, suivi de Le Discours du Grand Sommeil. Paris, Gallimard, 1925.
La Crucifixion. Paris, P. Morihien, 1946.
Le Chiffre Sept. Paris, Seghers, 1952.
Clair-Obscur. Monaco, Editions du Rocher, 1954.
Poèmes, 1916–1955. Paris, Gallimard, 1956.
Opéra, suivi de Plain-Chant. Paris, Stock, 1959.
Le Requiem. Paris, Gallimard, 1962.

Films

Le Sang d'un Poète. Monaco, Editions du Rocher, 1948.
L'Eternal Retour. Paris, Nouvelles Editions Françaises, 1948.
La Belle et la Bête. Paris, Editions du Pré-aux-Clercs, 1946.
Les Parents Terribles. Paris, Editions Le Monde Illustré, 1949.
Orphée. Paris, Editions André Bonne, 1951.
Le Testament d'Orphée. Monaco, Editions du Rocher, 1961.

Ballet

Parade. In Théâtre de Poche. Monaco, Editions du Rocher, 1955.
Le Boeuf sur le Toit. In Théâtre de Poche. Monaco, Editions du Rocher, 1955.
Les Mariés de la Tour Eiffel. In Théâtre I. Paris, Gallimard, 1948.
Romeo et Juliette. In Théâtre Complet. Paris, Grasset, 1957.

Murals

Chapelle Saint-Pierre. Villefranche-sur-Mer.
Mairie de Menton. Menton.
Chapelle Saint-Blaise des Simples. Milly-la-Forêt.

Critical Works and Commentary

Brown, Frederick. An Impersonation of Angels: A Biography of Jean Cocteau. New York, Viking Press, 1968.
Crosland, Margaret. Jean Cocteau. New York, Alfred A. Knopf, 1956.
Fowlie, Wallace. Jean Cocteau: The History of a Poet's Age. Bloomington, Indiana University Press, 1966.
Gilson, René. Jean Cocteau. Tr. Ciba Vaughan. New York, Crown, 1969.
Knapp, Bettina. Jean Cocteau. New York, Twayne, 1970.
Oxenhandler, Neal. Scandal and Parade: The Theater of Jean Cocteau. New Brunswick, Rutgers University Press, 1957.
Sprigge, Elizabeth, and Jean-Jacques Kihm. Jean Cocteau: The Man and the Mirror. New York, Coward-McCann, 1968.
Steegmuller, Francis. Cocteau, a Biography. Boston, Little, Brown, 1970.